Little Baby Steps™ to **Happiness**

STARBURST PUBLISHERS™

P.O. Box 4123 Lancaster, Pennsylvania 17604

Credits:

To schedule Author appearances write:
Author Appearances, Starburst Promotions, P.O. Box 4123
Lancaster, Pennsylvania 17604 or call (717) 293-0939.

Cover art by David Marty Design.
Scripture Quotations are from The Holy Bible:
King James Version, New International Version—Copyright 1984 by The International Bible Society and
published by Zondervan Bible Publishers.

We, the Publisher and Author, declare that to the best of our knowledge all material
(quoted or not) contained herein is accurate; and we shall not be held liable for the same.

"Little" Baby Steps to Happiness

First Printing, December 1996

ISBN: 0-914984-87-X
Library of Congress Catalog Number 96-68841

Printed in the United States of America.

"Little" Baby Steps to Happiness is an inspiring, witty, and insightful collection of quotes and affirmations from John Q. Baucom's book ***Baby Steps to Happiness*** (see ordering information at back of book) that will help you find happiness, one *"Little"* step at a time.

Take a moment to learn from the wisdom of Thomas Edison, Saint Francis of Assisi, Helen Keller, Robert Schuller, Mother Teresa, and others and "Make Your Life Happy."

Acknowledgments

The author thanks: LA, Shannon McKnight, and Bud Ragan for the formation of the early stages and the proposal of this book; LA, Shannon McKnight, Roy Glenn, Carol Rogers, Harrison, Clairalyn, and Jeremy for typing, editing, and proofreading; Roy Glenn, Bud Ragan, Carol Rogers, and Keppy for finding and editing quotes; Butch Simpson, Barry Wagner, Roy Glenn, Michael Alfono, Lois Smith, Edwinna Bierman, Benjamin, Chip, Valerie, and Sheri for inspiration.

Dedication

This book is dedicated to Shannon McKnight, without whom this work would not have been possible.

Begin where you are this very day. This is the perfect moment, the perfect place and the perfect opportunity. Take a baby step toward happiness.

A journey of a thousand miles must begin with a single step.

—Chinese Proverb

Momentum builds the moment you begin. Your own inertia can help propel you toward happiness. Take the first step of your journey today.

Remember that happiness is a way of travel— not a destination.

—Roy M. Goodman

**If you're not happy there's a reason—
what you're doing doesn't work.
Try something different today.
Take a baby step toward happiness.**

*To change one's life: start immediately.
Do it flamboyantly. No exceptions.*

—William James

Regardless of how much change is required, you can begin the journey today. Look one baby step ahead on the path of happiness.

Always bear in mind that your own resolution to succeed is more important than any one thing.
—Johann Wolfgang von Goethe

Little Baby Steps to Happiness

Your happiness is a consequence of the things you do. If what you're doing is not working, change it. The consequences will change as well.

Happiness is not a reward—it is a consequence.
—Robert G. Ingersoll

Doing the same thing over and expecting different results is one definition of insanity. Break away from the familiar path. Move toward happiness today.

Growth is the only evidence of life.
—John Henry, Cardinal Newman

You have an internal happiness thermostat. To change your happiness, you need to occasionally adjust the setting.

In making our decisions, we must use the brains that God has given us. But we must also use our hearts which He also gave us.

—Fulton Oursler

How much pain does it take for you to change? Develop a low threshold for unhappiness. Pain is a signal to change. Happiness is a signal to remain on the path.

The human mind can bear plenty of reality but not too much intermittent gloom.

—Margaret Drabble

If you had four weeks to live, how would you change your life? Whatever you would do then—do now. That's what's really important to you.

Once while St. Francis of Assisi was hoeing his garden, he was asked, "What would you do if you were suddenly to learn that you were to die at sunset today?" He replied, "I would finish hoeing my garden."

—Anonymous

Most people never live the life they imagined. Instead, others imagine and dream—and they chase what is given to them. Be different. Imagine your own life today.

To watch the corn grow, or the blossoms set;
to draw hard breath over the plowshare or spade;
to read, to think, to love, to pray, are the things that
make men happy.

—John Ruskin

Little Baby Steps to Happiness

**If you could have the life you honestly
desire, what would it be? Visualize that
life. Then pursue it, one baby step at a time.**

*Surely there is grandeur in knowing that in the
realm of thought, at least, you are without a chain;
that you have the right to explore all heights and all
depths; that there are no walls nor fences, nor
prohibited places, nor sacred corners in all the vast
expanse of thought . . .*

—Robert G. Ingersoll

People on their death beds are often blessed with crystal clear clarity. Don't wait till then to know what's really important. Visualize it today.

If a man hasn't discovered something that he will die for, he isn't fit to live.

—Martin Luther King, Jr.

To change your happiness, focus on what you can control. Think about it. What do you really have control over? That's where you focus.

It is not how many years we live but rather what we do with them.

—Evangeline Cory Booth

You can own your life. You've probably given ownership away to creditors, people, or what you consider to be "security." It's time to begin owning your life again— one baby step at a time.

Chase after money and security and your heart will never unclench. Care about people's approval and you will be their prisoner.

—Lao Tze

Create your own vision of the life you want to lead. Write about it. Imagine it. Plan for it. Begin on the path to happiness.

Where there is no vision, the people perish.
—Proverbs 29:18a

Don't live *for* the moment, live *in* the moment. Make the most of what is . . . one moment at a time.

Know the true value of time; snatch, seize, and enjoy every moment of it.
—Philip Dormer Stanhope, Lord Chesterfield

The past is gone. The future may never arrive. Live right now. This moment is yours. Make the most of it.

Lost, yesterday, somewhere between sunrise and sunset, two golden hours, each set with sixty diamond minutes. No reward is offered, for they are gone forever.

—Horace Mann

Little Baby Steps to Happiness

**What you want may be far different from
what you need. Do what you need to do.
You'll have far more happiness in the long
run.**

*Be very careful, then, how you live—not as unwise
but as wise, making the most of every opportunity . . . .*
—Ephesians 5:15-16a NIV

When your wants, needs and behaviors are aligned, you are living a congruent life. You then have a legitimate claim to happiness.

The spiritual life is first of all a life.
It is not merely something to be known and studied,
it is to be lived.

—Thomas Merton

Delaying gratification is not really putting off anything. It is investing in long-term rewards. One of those rewards is happiness.

Cast your bread upon the waters, for after many days you will find it again.

—Ecclesiastes 11:1 NIV

You will never be happier than you expect. To change your happiness, change your expectations.

Attempt the impossible in order to improve your work.

—Bette Davis

What you believe as true about yourself at the deepest level is your reality. To create permanent change in your life focus at this level.

For as he thinketh in his heart, so is he.

—Proverbs 23:7

If you sincerely believe you are worthy of happiness, you can experience it. Without this belief, happiness is impossible.

No man is happy who does not think himself so.
—Publilius Syrus

You live life with yourself, twenty-four hours a day for the rest of your life. Invest in liking yourself, your dreams, and your work.

Blessed is he who has found his work; let him ask no other blessedness. He has a work, a life-purpose; he has found it, and will follow it . . . Labor is life.
— Thomas Carlyle

You can have anything you want. But you can't have everything you want. Decide what is really important to you and pursue it.

With the help of my God, I shall leap over the wall.
—Book of Common Prayer

You will never achieve a goal that conflicts with your values. Determine your values before you set goals.

The soul that has no established aim loses itself.
—Michel de Montaigne

Little Baby Steps to Happiness

"Happiness," said Curly, in the movie, *City Slickers*, while holding up one finger,"is just one thing." You decide what that one thing is.

Life can never be wholly dark or futile once the key to its meaning is in our hands.

—J. B. Phillips

Focus on the purpose of your life. Talk about it. Discuss it. Write about it. Determine it. It makes all life more meaningful.

Many persons have a wrong idea of what constitutes true happiness. It is not attained through self-gratification, but through fidelity to a worthy purpose.

—Helen Keller

Have a reason to get out of bed each morning. Create a daily purpose for your life that excites passion within you. The passion will create energy.

To live successfully, everyone needs a purpose.
—George Sweeting

Life's work is not about the inheritance of money. It's your legacy, your values, your beliefs, and most of all your love.

I believe that unarmed truth and unconditional love will have the final word in reality.

—Martin Luther King, Jr.

Schedule an appointment with yourself weekly. During this time, do something purely for fun. It will keep you on the road to happiness.

The soul of one who loves God always swims in joy, always keeps a holiday, and is always in a mood for singing.

—St. John of the Cross

Each day it is important to schedule some pleasurable activity, even if it's only for five minutes. Introduce "mini-vacations" into your daily life.

There is a time for everything and a season for every activity under heaven: . . . a time to weep and a time to laugh, a time to mourn and a time to dance.

—Ecclesiastes 3:1,4 NIV

**Going to the dentist may be painful.
Many painful things are necessary.
Schedule necessary painful events.
A little pain now may save a lot later.**

*Although the world is full of suffering, it is full also
of the overcoming of it.*

—Helen Keller

**Be careful what you practice.
Practice anger, you'll become angry.
Practice happiness, you'll become happy.
What you practice you become.**

*Nobody ever mastered any skill except
through intensive, persistent and intelligent
practice. Practice it the right way.*

—Norman Vincent Peale

Your mind doesn't know the difference between that which is vividly imagined and that which is real. Visualize to realize.

Imagination is the air of the mind.

—Philip James Bailey

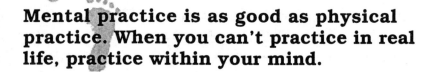

Mental practice is as good as physical practice. When you can't practice in real life, practice within your mind.

Imagination is more important than information.
—Albert Einstein

Don't sit around and wait for things to happen. Go get involved and happen to things.

If you see a good fight, get in it.

—Martin Luther King, Jr.

I've heard many people say "my marriage isn't working out." Marriages don't work. People do. Or they don't. Happen to life.

Action may not always bring happiness; but there is no happiness without action.

—Benjamin Disraeli

Money is like oxygen. The absence of it can create real problems. But the presence of it does not create happiness.

Money reveals where our interests lie; it can direct our attitudes: it ever exposes us to the danger of worshipping it; and it represents value. Money not only talks; it screams.

—Leslie B. Flynn

Money can pay your bills.
But it can't buy you happiness.

The bird of paradise alights only upon the hand that does not grasp.

—John Berry

Material objects fall into the category of deficiency needs. Focus away from deficits and toward the possibilities of happiness and peace of mind.

Whensoever a man desires anything inordinately, he is presently disquieted within himself.
—Thomas à Kempis

Happiness doesn't result from merely breathing. It is the by-product of living a full life in an honest and active way.

A man would do nothing if he waited until he could do it so well that no one would find fault with what he has done.

—John Henry, Cardinal Newman

You can't be a musician without practicing music. You can't be happy without practicing life. During practice things will not be perfect. Keep practicing.

Genius is 1% inspiration and 99% perspiration.
—Thomas Edison

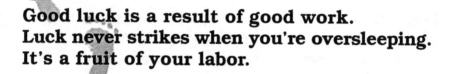

Good luck is a result of good work.
Luck never strikes when you're oversleeping.
It's a fruit of your labor.

I am a great believer in luck, and I find the harder I
work the more I have of it.

—Stephen Leacock

Genius is not from thought. It's thought followed by activity. Not in the furrow of the brow—but the sweat of the brow.

No one can arrive from being talented alone. God gives talent, work transforms talent into genius.
—Anna Pavlova

All great champions have one thing in common. It's not body type. It's not "natural talent." It's not race, gender, or ethnicity. It's work.

Destiny is not a matter of chance, it is a matter of choice; it is not a thing to be waited for, it is a thing to be achieved.

—William Jennings Bryan

Love to win more than you hate to lose. It will propel you to keep on going and eventually win.

Success is not so much achievement as achieving. Refuse to join the cautious crowd that plays not to lose; play to win.

—David J. Mahoney

Failure only occurs when you quit learning or quit doing. Everything else is a learning experience.

Apparent failure may hold in its rough shell the germs of a success that will blossom in time, and bear fruit throughout eternity.

—Frances Ellen Watkins Hayer

Mistakes are the tuition we pay on the path to success.

In the Divine Order what generally seems at first a failure may be a vestibule for a future success.
—Bishop Fulton J. Sheen

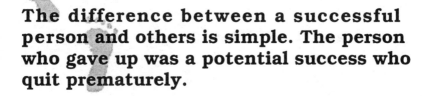

The difference between a successful person and others is simple. The person who gave up was a potential success who quit prematurely.

Remember when life's path is steep to keep your mind open.

—Horace

**Learn to deal with suffering.
It's there purposely for you to learn.
Don't miss out on the opportunity.**

*Life is not all fun and easy going. Far from it; there
are many rough times. But, sadly, we too often let
the hard times dull our enthusiasm. And that is
dangerous, if not fatal, to our lives.*

—Norman Vincent Peale

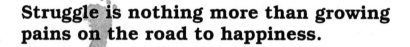

Struggle is nothing more than growing pains on the road to happiness.

A failure is a man who has blundered, but is not able to cash in on the experience.

—Elbert Hubbard

There is pain in childbirth. But the outcome is miraculous new life. Most other miracles require similar pain.

No pain, no palm; no thorns, no throne; no gall, no glory; no cross, no crown.

—William Penn

There are responses in your life that you are not happy with. To change your responses, change your messages.

For whatsoever a man soweth, that shall he also reap.

—Galatians 6:7

Self-control is the only true control that is possible.

He that is slow to anger is better than the mighty; and he that ruleth his spirit, than he that taketh a city.
—Proverbs 16:32

You can't control the weather. You can't control traffic. You can't control other people. You *can* control the way you react to each of those.

How much more grievous are the consequences of anger than the causes of it!

—Marcus Aurelius

Most people spend too much time obsessing about things over which they have no control, while ignoring the ones over which they do—themselves.

God grant me the serenity to accept the things I cannot change, Courage to change the things I can and Wisdom to know the difference.
                              —Alcoholics Anonymous Serenity Prayer

The moment you accept complete responsibility for your life circumstances, is the moment you change them.

It matters not how straight the gate, How charged with punishments the scrolls, I am the master of my fate: I am the captain of my soul.

—W. E. Henley

You are not what other people think of you. You are you. Their thoughts are their thoughts. They are two different things, that seldom coincide.

No one can make you feel inferior without your consent.
—Eleanor Roosevelt

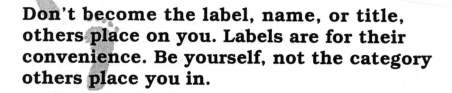

Don't become the label, name, or title, others place on you. Labels are for their convenience. Be yourself, not the category others place you in.

When you are content to be simply yourself and don't compare or compete, everybody will respect you.

—Lao Tze

To be happy is to be independent of the opinion, disapproval or approval of others.

Love yourself first and everything else falls into line. You really have to love yourself to get anything done in this world.

—Lucille Ball

Little Baby Steps to Happiness

**Don't be concerned about what others say.
Be concerned about what you are.**

*Do not worry about people not knowing your ability:
worry about not having it.*

—Confucius

You can't control your thoughts. However, you can choose those you focus on.

Finally, brothers, whatever is true, whatever is noble, whatever is right, whatever is pure, whatever is lovely, whatever is admirable—if anything is excellent or praiseworthy—think about such things.

—Philippians 4:8 NIV

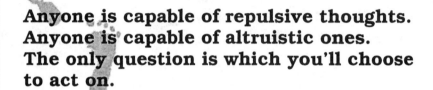

**Anyone is capable of repulsive thoughts.
Anyone is capable of altruistic ones.
The only question is which you'll choose
to act on.**

*Thoughts are energy. And you can make your world
or break your world by thinking.*

—Susan Taylor

Don't aim for normal. Be abnormal. Aim for the extraordinary.

Keep your feet on the ground, but let your heart soar as high as it will. Refuse to be average or to surrender to the chill of your spiritual environment.

—A.W. Tozer

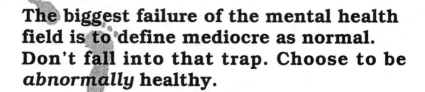

The biggest failure of the mental health field is to define mediocre as normal. Don't fall into that trap. Choose to be *abnormally* healthy.

The general tendency of things throughout the world is to render mediocrity the ascendant power among mankind.

—John Stuart Mill

You are capable of achieving far more than what we have come to define as normal. Break away from the boredom. Achieve your potential.

You must do the thing you think you cannot do.
—Eleanor Roosevelt

Love people—not things. The tendency toward the opposite will always lead toward misery.

Do not store up for yourselves treasures on earth, where moth and rust destroy, and where thieves break in and steal.

—Matthew 6:19 NIV

Little Baby Steps to Happiness

The greatest joy you'll experience will come from relationships with others. But so will the greatest sadness. You can't have one without the other.

God evidently does not intend us all to be rich, or powerful or great, but He does intend us all to be friendly.

—Ralph Waldo Emerson

A theory is how something should be. Reality is how it is. Those are often entirely different.

We live in a fantasy world, a world of illusion. The great task in life is to find reality.

—Iris Murdoch

Theory can prove a bumble bee can't fly. It's a good thing bumble bees can't understand theory.

Dear friend, theory is all gray, and the golden tree of life is green.

—Johann Wolfgang von Goethe

**In 1976, I easily ran a marathon.
Then I read how difficult it is.
I didn't complete the next one.
I threw the book away.**

*If you think you can win, you can win.
Faith is necessary to victory.*

—William Hazlitt

Don't see life as you want it to be.
Don't see it as you think it should be.
See things as they are.

The real world is not easy to live in. It is rough;
it is slippery. Without the most clear-eyed adjustments
we fall and get crushed.

—Clarence Day

**Open your eyes. Blink twice. Wake up.
Look around you. See life as it is—
not how you want it to be.**

*Life is, for the most part, the way we see it.
So, when life's not fair—it may be time to check your
focus. Change your seeing to change your scene.*
                                        —Robert Schuller

True. A lady got a love letter. Rather than enjoying it, she complained about the ugly envelope. See the forest as well as the trees.

There is no greater disaster in the spiritual life than to be immersed in unreality, for life is maintained and nourished in us by our vital relation with realities outside and above us.

—Thomas Merton

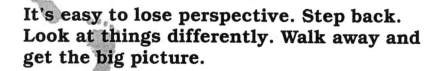

It's easy to lose perspective. Step back. Look at things differently. Walk away and get the big picture.

Do your work, then step back. The only path to serenity.

—Lao Tze

**Put people first. Value humanity.
Find someone to love more than yourself.
Happiness will then find you.**

*God loves you. Love one another as he loves you.
Love is sharing. Love is giving the best we have.*
—Mother Teresa

An insult is only empty words unless you believe it. But so is a compliment.

If you don't run your own life, somebody else will.
—John Atkinson

It takes two people to dance. It takes two people to argue. No one can offend you without your permission. Quit giving it.

True guilt is guilt at the obligation one owes to oneself, to actualize oneself. False guilt is guilt felt at not being what other people feel one ought to be or assume that one is.

—R.D. Laing

Be free of petty conflicts. Don't argue. Don't try to convince someone else they're wrong. Simply don't be there.

There is in stillness oft a magic power to calm the breast when struggling passions lower, Touched by its influence, in the soul arise diviner feelings, kindred with the skies.

—John Henry, Cardinal Newman

**A gift is not yours unless you accept it.
An insult is not yours unless you believe it.
A disagreement does not occur unless you
participate.**

*And thou shalt take no gift: for the gift blindeth the
wise, and perverteth the words of the righteous.*
—Exodus 23:8

Just because something looks good, doesn't mean it is. Trojan horses often pack surprises. If it looks too good to be true, it is.

I fear the Greeks, even when they bring gifts.

—Vergil

There are many distractions on the road to happiness. But there are on any trip. Look at the distractions as opportunities to refuel your tank.

The person who makes a success of living is the one who sees his goal steadily and aims for it unswervingly.

—Cecil B. DeMille

Most people are socialized to give control of their life to others. Who's in charge of your life? Who's driving your bus? Take control.

The question is . . . Who's to be master?

—Lewis Carroll

There may be times when you're tired of driving your own bus. Have a few designated drivers. But ensure you can trust them.

A friend is someone who will make us do what we can when we are saying we can't.

—Ralph Waldo Emerson

You can learn to say "no" when necessary, in a diplomatic and assertive way. Think about it. Practice it. Rehearse it with others. It's an important step.

Consider well what your strength is equal to, and what exceeds your ability.

—Horace

Know your limits. Respect them. Often your limit is your subconscious saying, "Give me a break."

Be master of your petty annoyances and conserve your energies for the big worthwhile things.

—Robert Service

When a cargo ship reaches harbor, it unloads. You may occasionally need to do the same thing. Carrying around old baggage can slow you on the journey.

It will be a great thing for the human soul when it finally stops worshipping backwards.
—Charlotte Perkins Stetson Gilman

The best revenge is happiness. When somebody purposely tries to hurt you, really get even. Be happy anyway.

The best manner of avenging ourselves is by not resembling him who has injured us.

—Jane Porter

There will be times when people want to hurt you just because you're there. Don't try to understand it. Just don't be there.

Stones and sticks are thrown only at fruit bearing trees.

—Sa'adi

Your interpretation of an event is far more powerful than the event itself. One man's tragedy is another's inconvenience. Interpret wisely.

If you are distressed by anything external, the pain is not due to the thing itself, but to your own estimate of it; and this you have the power to revoke at any moment.

—Marcus Aurelius

**Would you rather be right or happy?
Most people say both. It won't happen.
Choose happiness today.**

*A life spent in making mistakes is not only more
honorable but more useful than a life spent in doing
nothing.*

—George Bernard Shaw

**Don't worry about being perfect.
Just be yourself. By doing so you'll be
perfectly you. Imperfect.**

*The man who makes no mistakes does not usually
make anything.*

—Edward J. Phelps

Go out of your way to find humor in everyday life. Laughter is your mind's way of giving itself a tune-up.

Humor is an affirmation of dignity, a declaration of man's superiority to all that befalls him.
—Romain Gary, *Promise at Dawn*

People who'd rather be right than happy are perfectionists. They experience more headaches, ulcers, unemployment, cancer, and suicide. Me? I'd rather be happy.

The essence of being human is that one does not seek perfection.

—George Orwell

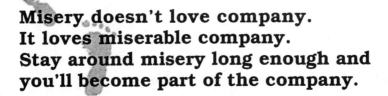

**Misery doesn't love company.
It loves miserable company.
Stay around misery long enough and
you'll become part of the company.**

*I don't believe there is a hopeless situation for which
there isn't a hopeful alternative.*

—Norman Vincent Peale

Misery has a magnetic appeal. Turn your end of the misery magnet around. Be repelled by misery, and attracted by its polar opposite—happiness.

He who loves a quarrel loves sin; he who builds a high gate invites destruction. A man of perverse heart does not prosper; he whose tongue is deceitful falls into trouble . . . A cheerful heart is good medicine, but a crushed spirit dries up the bones.
—Proverbs 17:19-20, 22 NIV

Quicksand is not quick. It slowly overwhelms you 'til you're consumed. Misery has a quicksand-like appeal. Don't be fooled by it.

. . . so far as we are narrow-spirited we're uneasy. Prejudices, jealousies, and suspicions make the soul miserable.

—George Whitefield

Happiness loves company. But it loves happy company. Sometimes you have to look a while. But it's worth it.

Here we write well when we expose frauds and hypocrites. We are great at counting warts and blemishes and weighing feet of clay. In expressing love, we belong among the undeveloped countries.
—Saul Bellow

You won't necessarily be popular if you're happy. Happiness is one goal. Popularity is another. Make happiness your goal.

There is little difference in people, but that little difference makes a big difference. That little difference is attitude. The big difference is whether it is positive or negative.

—Clement Stone

Don't aspire to the status quo. The status quo is miserable. Instead be happy.

It has always been a mystery to me how men can feel themselves honored by the humiliation of their fellow beings.

—Mahatma Gandhi

The past does not equal your present.
The present does not equal your future.
The future is filled with possibilities.
Happiness awaits you. Claim it.

No man who is correctly informed as to the past will be disposed to take a morose or desponding view of the present.

— Thomas Babington Macaulay

Happiness is not a thing. You'll never own it. It's like your ideal weight. Happiness requires attention. Or you lose it.

Happiness depends upon ourselves.

—Fyodor Dostoyevsky

Happiness is not: A car, a nose job or money. You'll never own it. You live it. One Baby Step at a time.

There is only one success . . . to be able to spend your life in your own way.

—Christopher Morley

Success is one goal. Money is a second goal. Happiness is a third. Choose happiness and the others will follow.

I do not pray for success. I pray for faithfulness.
—Mother Teresa

If money is your goal you will earn it.
If success is your passion, you'll experience it.
Neither will necessarily result in happiness.

Watch out! Be on your guard against all kinds of greed; a man's life does not consist in the abundance of his possessions.

—Luke 12:15 NIV

Most Americans think happiness is the three "R's." Recognition. Remuneration. Respect of peers. Also, most Americans are unhappy. Don't be like most Americans. Be happy.

The mass of men lead lives of quiet desperation. What is called resignation is confirmed desperation.
—Henry David Thoreau

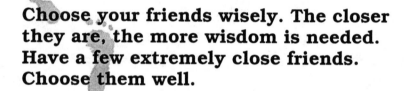

Choose your friends wisely. The closer they are, the more wisdom is needed. Have a few extremely close friends. Choose them well.

Be devoted to one another in brotherly love.

—Romans 12:10a NIV

Have many acquaintances. Tell them little, other than hello. Have a few intimate friends. Tell them everything, after you say hello.

Let us look at each other without mistrust, meet each other without fear, talk with each other without surrendering principle.

—Pope John XXIII

Have one very special friend. This is the person you can tell virtually anything about yourself and she'll love you anyway.

True friendship is like sound health; the value of it is seldom known until it be lost.

—Charles Caleb Colton

Never try to join a club that doesn't want you as a member. Even if you're admitted you wouldn't be welcomed.

Men cannot be brothers if they are not humble. It is pride, no matter how legitimate it may seem to be, that provokes tension, and struggles for prestige, for predominance, colonialism, egoism. That is, pride disrupts brotherhood.

—Pope Paul VI

Membership in a community is important. Acceptance is more important. Be part of a community. But only one that accepts you as a member.

There can be no vulnerability without risk; there can be no community without vulnerability; there can be no peace, and ultimately no life, without community.

—M. Scott Peck

**The need for "belonging" comes after safety and survival. It's basic.
Find a group to belong to—but only one where you are loved.**

Many waters cannot quench love, neither can the floods drown it.

—Song of Solomon 8:7a

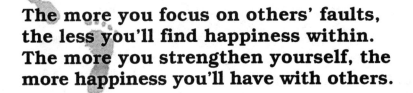

The more you focus on others' faults, the less you'll find happiness within. The more you strengthen yourself, the more happiness you'll have with others.

I have had more trouble with myself than with any other man.

—D.L. Moody

To help yourself, help others. Find someone worse off than you, and help them. It's a major Baby Step on the road to happiness.

There is always something radically wrong with a situation in which those who have too much are indifferent to others who have too little. This is often a sign that the society in which it occurs is hastening to its ruin.

—Billy Graham

**Reach out to people. Offer them help.
If you do, they'll ultimately reach back.**

*Down in their hearts, wise men know this truth: The
only way to help yourself is to help others.*
—Elbert Hubbard

Nothing feels as good as helping heal another's pain. When you do this each of your lives are enriched.

Each of us can expect astonishing results when we seize the opportunity to help someone else. And in the right spirit, it makes us feel good.

—Norman Vincent Peale

Accept first. Understand later.

A friend is one to whom one may pour out all the contents of one's heart, chaff and grain together, knowing that the gentlest of hands will take and sift it, keep what is worth keeping, and with a breath of kindness, blow the rest away.

—Anonymous

Forget about understanding. Let's be stupid together. It's one of the Baby Steps on the road to happiness.

A gentle answer turns away wrath, but a harsh word stirs up anger.

—Proverbs 15:1 NIV

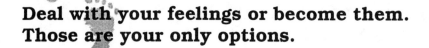

Deal with your feelings or become them. Those are your only options.

Cherish your own emotions and never undervalue them.

—Robert Henri

Talk about your anger, and you won't become angry. Talk about your fear and you won't become frightened. Talk about your feelings or become them.

The fiercest people are not those who are bold, but those who are frightened.

—Sydney J. Harris

You have a finite supply of daily emotional energy. How you expend it is up to you. Resolve today to use it for happiness only.

We have no time but Present Time; therefore prize your time for your soul's sake.

—George Fox

Motion controls emotion. You can change the way you feel by changing what you do with your body.

Nothing lifts me out of a bad mood better than a hard workout on my treadmill. It never fails: to us, exercise is nothing short of a miracle.

—Cher

Jump-start yourself out of a bad mood by twenty to thirty minutes of vigorous aerobic exercise: The world's most powerful anti-depressant.

If you would add a little to a little and do this often, soon the little will become great.

—Hesiod

The key that unlocks creativity is not in thought. It's in your legs. Move them! Vigorously! It generates the mind as well as the body.

Whatever you can do, or dream you can, begin it. Boldness has genius, power and magic in it.
—Johann Wolfgang von Goethe

Little Baby Steps to Happiness

**When you need a crutch, use it.
After your leg heals, discard it.
Dependency is hanging onto the
crutch long after your leg is healed.**

*No bird soars too high, if he soars with his own
wings.*

—William Blake

**Reject dependency in any form.
Don't be dependent on another.
And don't let another be dependent
on you.**

*No one can build his security upon the nobleness
of another person.*

—Willa Cather

Love is not dependency. Love frees dependency. Love occurs when two independent people join together and become stronger due to the other's presence.

A friend is a gift you give yourself.

—Robert Louis Stevenson

Depersonalize. 95% of the things that happen around you aren't personal. The other 5% you need to ignore.

We cannot control the evil tongues of others; but a good life enables us to disregard them.
—Cato the Elder

Scientists tell us 88% of the things you worry about never happen. Probably another 11% are outside of your control. Focus on the 1% you can change.

Happiness makes up in height for what it lacks in length.

—Robert Frost

Take almost nothing personally. Detach. Back up. Look again. It usually isn't about you at all. Then refocus on what is really important.

To be happy, we must not be too concerned with others.
—Albert Camus

"Don't worry. Be happy. . ." Worry has never solved anything. But it has made many problems worse.

For I have learned to be content whatever the circumstances.
—Philippians 4:11b NIV

Some scientists say 85% of all illness is due to stress-related worry. Want to reduce your medical expenses by 85%? Don't worry. Be happy.

Worry affects circulation, the heart and the glands, the whole nervous system and profoundly affects the heart. I have never known a man who died from overwork, but many who died from doubt.
—Charles H. Mayo

Program yourself for daily happiness. Listen to inspirational tapes. Go for a brisk walk. Find three things to laugh about—all before 7 a.m. Do happiness!

To fill the hour—that is happiness; to fill the hour, and leave no crevice for a repentance or an approval.
—Ralph Waldo Emerson

**Laugh daily. Guard your time.
Sleep deeply but briefly. Drink plenty
of water. Exercise vigorously.
Love someone. Pray. Get inspired daily.
Create balance.**

*Continual moderation is better than fits of
abstinence interspersed with occasional
excesses.*

—St. Francis De Sales

Have at least three things in your life you feel passionate about. Diversify.

Never to be completely idle, but either be reading, or writing, or praying, or meditating, or working at something useful for all in common.

—Thomas à Kempis

Diversify to the point that one part of your life complements and strengthens the other just as a group working together creates a team.

If we are to achieve a richer culture, rich in contrasting values, we must recognize the whole gamut of human potentialities, and so weave a less arbitrary social fabric, one in which each diverse human gift will find a fitting place.

—Margaret Mead

Simplify your life and increase your happiness. To the degree you do the first, you'll concurrently accomplish the second.

He who would travel happily must travel light.
—Robert Frost

**Go against the modern flow.
Simplify your life.**

I have just three things to teach: Simplicity, patience, compassion. These three are your greatest treasures.
—Lao Tze

A cluttered life is like a cluttered closet. It's aggravating 'til you straighten things out. Simplify.

Our life is frittered away by detail . . . Simplify, simplify.
—Henry David Thoreau

Pray daily with intensity.
Then listen with equal intensity.

Prayer is a sacrifice of adoration as well as a direct communion with God through which we penetrate the sanctuary of heaven, and admitted to God's presence, we question him about His promises.
—John Calvin

For happiness to bloom in your garden, fertilize it with daily quiet time.

The word meditation is rather an abused word . . . It would be much better to use the words "quiet time," in which a person shuts out the noise of the world, enters into himself and judges himself not by his press clippings, but how he stands with God.

—Bishop Fulton J. Sheen

**Prayer can change your life.
But only if you pray about it!**

*Prayer is a special exercise of faith. Faith makes the
prayer acceptable because it believes that either the
prayer will be answered, or that something
better will be given.*

—Martin Luther

It's not going to a church that makes you a Christian. It's being Christ-like. Spiritual is as spiritual does.

Do all the good you can, By all the means you can.
In all the ways you can, In all the places you can,
At all the times you can, To all the people you can,
As long as you ever can.

—John Wesley

A high degree of "spiritual fusion" is found in high achievers. They incorporate spirituality into everyday life. Spiritual is as spiritual does.

Science can point out dangers, but science cannot turn the direction of minds and hearts. That is the province of spiritual powers within and without our very beings—powers that are the mysteries of life itself.
—Oren Lyons

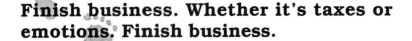

Finish business. Whether it's taxes or emotions. Finish business.

The past must be abandoned to God's mercy, the present to our fidelity, the future to divine providence.

—St. Francis De Sales

Life begs for closure. A telephone call on hold begs to be answered. A tune seeks to be completed. Get closure in all things.

Why doesn't the past decently bury itself instead of sitting waiting to be admired by the present?
—D. H. Lawrence

I have grieved at every funeral I've attended. I've grieved far more for the one's I haven't attended. Finish business.

The past can be a rudder that guides you or an anchor that hinders you. Leave your mistakes with God and look to the future by faith.

—Warren Wiersbe

Finish business. Say hello. Say good-bye. Laugh when there's joy. Grieve when there's sadness. Forgive. Love. Let go. Finish business.

This one thing I do, forgetting those things which are behind, and reaching forth unto those things which are before. I press toward the mark.
—Philippians 3:13b-14a

People need rituals. There are birthday, anniversary, birth, death, happy, sad, festive, annual, monthly, weekly—rituals. We need them. Develop rituals for your life.

If I do not spend a reasonable amount of time in meditation early in the morning, then I feel a physical discomfort. It is worse than having forgotten to brush my teeth.

—Archbishop Desmond Tutu

Enjoy life. This is not a dress rehearsal. It's real. It's important. It's not practice. Enjoy life.

Do not boast about tomorrow, for you do not know what a day may bring forth.

—Proverbs 27:1 NIV

Some have come close to living their potential. But very few. Ask more from yourself. More joy. More intensity. More life.

Let your life lightly dance on the edges of time like dew on the tip of a leaf.

—Sir Rabindranath Tagore

If you were 100 years old, looking back at your life, what would you then regret? Don't wait to make these changes. Do it now.

Let us therefore make every effort to do what leads to peace.

—Romans 14:19a NIV

Nobody is buried with the epitaph: ". . . she maintained her ideal weight . . ." or ". . . he had a good credit rating . . . ." Live for what's really important.

Peace be within thy walls, and prosperity within thy palaces.

—Psalm 122:7

"Little" Baby Steps to Happiness
—John Q. Baucom

Inspiring, witty and insightful, this portable collection of quotes and affirmations from **Baby Steps to Happiness** will encourage Happiness one *"little"* footstep at a time. This book is the perfect personal "cheerleader."

(trade paper) ISBN 091498487X **$6.95**

Baby Steps to Happiness
—John Q. Baucom

Subtitled: *52 Inspiring Ways to Make Your Life Happy.* This unique 52-step approach will enable the reader to focus on small steps that bring practical and proven change. The author encourages the reader to take responsibility for the Happiness that only he can find. Chapter titles, such as, *Have a Reason to Get Out of Bed, Deal with Your Feelings or Become Them, Would You Rather Be Right or Happy?,* and *Love To Win More Than You Hate to Lose* give insight and encouragement on the road to happiness.

(trade paper) ISBN 0914984861 **$12.95**

God's Vitamin "C" for the Spirit
—Kathy Collard Miller & D. Larry Miller

Subtitled: *"Tug-at-the-Heart" Stories to Fortify and Enrich Your Life.*
Includes inspiring stories and anecdotes that emphasize Christian ideals and values by some of the most-loved Christian writers. Topics include: Love, Family Life, Faith and Trust, Prayer and Marriage.

(trade paper) ISBN 0914984837 **$12.95**

God's Chewable Vitamin "C" for the Spirit

Subtitled: *A Dose of God's Wisdom One Bite at a Time.* A collection of inspirational quotes and Scriptures by many of your favorite Christian speakers and writers. It will motivate your life and inspire your spirit. You will *chew* on every *bite* of **God's Chewable Vitamin "C" for the Spirit.**

(trade paper) ISBN 0914984845 **$6.95**

God's Vitamin "C" for the Christmas Spirit

—Kathy Collard Miller & D. Larry Miller

Subtitled: *"Tug-at-the-Heart" Traditions and Inspirations to Warm the Heart.*
This gift book includes a variety of *"Heart-Tugging"* thoughts, stories, poetry, recipes, songs and ideas from some of the most-loved Christian writers and speakers.

(hardcover) ISBN 0914984853 **$14.95**

Purchasing Information: Books are available from your favorite Bookstore, either from current stock or special order. To assist bookstore in locating your selection be sure to give title, author, and ISBN #. If unable to purchase from the bookstore you may order direct from STARBURST PUBLISHERS. When ordering enclose full payment plus $3.00 for shipping and handling ($4.00 if Canada or Overseas). Payment in US Funds only. Please allow two to three weeks minimum (longer overseas) for delivery. Make checks payable to and mail to STARBURST PUBLISHERS, P.O. Box 4123, LANCASTER, PA 17604. Credit card orders may also be placed by calling 1-800-441-1456 (credit card orders only), Mon-Fri, 8 a.m. – 5 p.m. Eastern Time. **Prices subject to change without notice.** Catalog available for a 9 x 12 self-addressed envelope with 4 first-class stamps. 08-96